Saad AlSogair is an angel investor, mentor, and advisor from Khobar, Saudi Arabia. He has participated in over 400 early-stage startups including Ripple, Calm, Grove Collaborative, and Dollar Shave Club.

After reviewing thousands of pitch decks, he began to pick up common and costly mistakes frequently made by entrepreneurs that hurt their chances with investors. AlSogair saw this as an opportunity to give back and make a difference.

His book, **Your Idea, Their Money: The Entrepreneur's Guide to Closing Rounds**, serves as a handbook for entrepreneurs looking to land their first investors.

Dear first-time entrepreneur,
You've got this!

Saad AlSogair

YOUR IDEA, THEIR MONEY

THE ENTREPRENEUR'S GUIDE
TO CLOSING ROUNDS

AUSTIN MACAULEY PUBLISHERS™

LONDON • CAMBRIDGE • NEW YORK • SHARJAH

Copyright © Saad AlSogair 2021

ISBN – 9789948834229 – (Paperback)
ISBN – 9789948834212 – (E-Book)

Application Number: MC-10-01-0113361
Age Classification: E

First Published 2021
AUSTIN MACAULEY PUBLISHERS FZE
Sharjah Publishing City
P.O Box [519201]
Sharjah, UAE

www.austinmacauley.ae
+971 655 95 202

66

Serious player – Saad moves quickly and is a delight to work with.

– Gil Penchina, Founder, Flight VC on AngelList

99

66

Saad has been a great investor, always eager to help out when he can.

– Mike Norman, President, Wefunder

99

TABLE OF CONTENTS

INTRODUCTION

The world of startup funding can be a scary place for optimistic entrepreneurs. Early failure is almost guaranteed for many of them, and oftentimes it can be attributed to a shortage of funding money. On the other side of the coin – presenting a well-researched and carefully prepared funding presentation to investors, and having them accept your proposal – that is an exciting and rewarding experience. *Your Idea, Their Money* is an encyclopedia for aspiring entrepreneurs and business owners who are working to fund their ventures.

This book covers the necessary topics to raise funds as an entrepreneur, including the definitions of financial terms, common misconceptions regarding investors and startups, and guidance for choosing the best method of fundraising for your project.

The basic concept that many entrepreneurs fail to understand is the difference between investor and entrepreneur mind-sets. The two parties view money through different lenses. Business owners search for funds as a means to get their operation off the ground. An investor only supplies money when a profit can be realized. As an entrepreneur, you must understand both sides of this dynamic to effectively pitch to investors and raise funds.

It is essential to recognize and categorize the current stage of the funding of your startup, in order to engineer a custom strategy to target the correct investors. Startups are split up into four types: self-funding, seed capital, venture, and IPO. All are explained in depth in this book.

After a startup is categorized, the next step is to identify funding sources and create a plan of attack. Personal preference holds a great deal of weight in this decision, but many entrepreneurs make poor choices at this point. Typically, business owners target the hardest methods of acquiring funds, and thus limit their fundraising potential. If the entrepreneur will widen their vision and knowledge, they can increase the likelihood of increased funding.

Equity and debt financing comprise the two major methods of funding covered in this book. These methods are split into e even options, which means that entrepreneurs are provided with more paths than they may initially realize. Choosing the right method is critical, and entrepreneurs reading this book will be equipped with the tools required to make the best decision possible.

Being the leader and founder of a business venture comes with its own unique set of responsibilities. These responsibilities are intertwined and exert a great impact on the financial viability and success of a startup. Every decision you make affects the present and future state of your company. If you fully understand those complex responsibilities and their importance, it will be easier to create a powerful and effective business plan. The business plan is arguably the most significant aspect of a startup, so a good portion of this book has been dedicated to the process of creating a plan. A solid business plan must be developed before any financial funding can be realized. Without it, startups fail to gain traction and soon crumble.

Another important skill that this book illustrates is the art of pitching a business idea. With their business plan in mind, an entrepreneur can use pitches as a means to gain investors and business partners.

The two pitch techniques explained in this book are the elevator pitch and the pitch deck. The elevator pitch is a short and sweet speech, to persuade the listener in two minutes or less and it can be used in a variety of situations. The pitch deck is more formal and typically consists of a speech reinforced by a PowerPoint presentation. By following the rough template provided in this book, entrepreneurs can use the pitch deck to seal the deal with investors.

After learning the aforementioned terms and techniques, and completing all of the requirements, entrepreneurs will be well prepared to put their plan into action. The final half of this book outlines the steps required for entrepreneurs to land investments. Using the skills, techniques, and terms introduced earlier in the book, business owners can use this outline as a guide to nail their fundraising and take their startup to the next level. It is a fantastic feeling to land that critical funding that will propel your business forward.

Startups aren't guaranteed to succeed, and more often than not they fail rather quickly. Most entrepreneurs simply take the wrong approach to start a business, and it eventually backfires. The shortcomings range from disorganization or corner-cutting to a simple lack of education on key subjects, and leave many new business owners ill-equipped to survive the world of fundraising. *Your Idea, Their Money* looks to change that model, and make you a successful fundraiser.

In addition to poor technique, many entrepreneurs lack

the mind-set that separates the successful from the unsuccessful. Everyone can find success, if they equip themselves with the proper fundamentals, and utilize them properly. Yes, an undeterred drive to succeed is absolutely crucial, but a willingness to fail and learn from your failures is equally important.

Perhaps the most important and beneficial concept covered in this book is contemplation and reflection. That is the process by which you learn from your mistakes, and determine ways not to repeat them. Every technique in this book has been used by countless entrepreneurs and business owners to gain success, but without assessing the results, nothing can be learned. As the book suggests, always take the time to reflect on your outcomes, whether positive or negative.

Whether you're an aspiring entrepreneur, a new business owner, or even a success story, this book will be of great benefit to you. The ideas and concepts covered provide anyone with a great chance of landing investors, regardless of their education or background. If you want to increase your financial knowledge and take your startup to the top, this is the book for you!

BOOK SUMMARY

The single largest problem that entrepreneurs face is fundraising. Aspiring business owners and grand product ideas are plentiful, but the sad reality is that most startups fail to get off of the ground.

Your Idea, Their Money is aimed at those who struggle to find and close the deal to get investors for their startups. While most entrepreneurs have the drive, few actually possess the skills, terminology, and knowledge required to effectively raise funds. In this book, Saad AlSogair covers not only the basics of entrepreneurship but provides business owners with a blueprint for how to impress investors.

Entrepreneurs who pick up this guide will learn about the investors' mind-set, the different means of investment, how to build executive summaries and business plans, how to put together pitches, and much more. *Your Idea, Their Money* is indispensable for any entrepreneur or business owner who is unsure of their next steps.

Creating a business is no easy task. Stats tell us that only half of new businesses complete their fifth year and only 30% make it to the tenth.

For startups, failure is almost a dominant force. Despite all that, hundreds of entrepreneurs pursue this path. Why? Because it's extremely rewarding. You learn a lot along the way. Getting started, then funded and running profitable operations is a daunting task, however. It is not for the faint-hearted.

After you get your business off the ground, one of the

vital tasks before you is to secure funds. Also called "startup capital," this is simply the seed money any entrepreneur raises for their business.

Luckily, there are many ways you can fund or raise capital for your business. This book is all about how to acquire those funds. The main challenge is to choose the right source of funding. Each source of funding must be sought and handled differently, and each has its advantages and disadvantages. The most important factor in the success of your fundraising effort is to appreciate your "understanding gap." You have to understand how investors and other funding sources like banks think—particularly, how they perceive your risk/reward profile.

Becoming interested in your startup and wanting to fund it are two completely different things in the mind of a potential investor. You as an entrepreneur need to be able to differentiate and quickly identify which case is on the table. With that recognition, you should work on which investor you need to approach and when.

As an entrepreneur, you want the easiest and fastest way to funding. At the same time, you need to understand your preferences for entering such an arrangement. Like it or not, it's most likely true that your company growth will be easier with funding.

It is hard to appreciate the feeling that accompanies a handshake at the end of a successful funding meeting. It requires a lot of preparation and work to reach that point, but when you have just secured the funds that will take your company to the next level – I guarantee that you will have a big smile on your face.

Funding is a challenge but it has a big payoff!

THE FUNDING OPTIONS

PART

1

WHY DO YOU NEED FUNDING?
CAN YOU DO WITHOUT IT?

Many consider funding to be one of the vital stages in the startup journey. Getting external or venture funding seems to be the ultimate path to success. But can you do without it? Should you do without it? Well, there is no easy answer, but the truth is that an investor-free startup is beneficial in many ways. It provides you with full ownership, better control of your budget and business plans, and complete independence on just how the business should evolve or transform. You also get a better focus on your customers, since you have no other stakeholders.

However, a startup without external funding has its own limitations. Sooner or later you will face challenges because of resource constraints. Your risk appetite is lower and growth can be really slow. In many cases investors bring extensive experience to help your startup succeed. Their involvement in business management can add real value. They may help get things done faster and easier. Lack of experience in the market can be telling, as many entrepreneurs resort to "hit or miss" tactics.

Investors and entrepreneurs are completely different, but this obvious reality may elude us at first. An entrepreneur is characterized by knowledge, passion, and the persistence to create a profitable enterprise. They are out there when they realize the risk of failure, the dog-eat-dog competition that they face, and the demands of a relentless market. An investor enters the picture only where they're needed (or let's say, where there is potential to profit). An investor sees a business as having potential when it can grow two- or threefold or more if provided with additional investment, thereby generating guaranteed returns. For an investor, it's best to be in a return-generating position. The higher the return, the better.

There is a considerable overlap between an investor and entrepreneur, but the fact remains – they are different. When running a business, the differences can manifest very quickly. Whatever you do, make sure you optimize the management of business demands, funds, and daily operations.

When starting up, the most important thing in your

favor is a sound product or service. What you offer has to solve a real problem for a group of consumers. Investors are interested in finding a solid product-market fit, and look toward situations where monetization is the natural next step. The product or service should be able to meet real customer needs, in a way that is better than those products or services offered by existing players (if there are any). It's worth mentioning Dan Olsen's The Lean Product Playbook. Olsen proposes a six-step framework called the "lean product process" which includes:

- Determine your target customer
- Identify underserved customer needs
- Define your value proposition
- Specify your minimum viable product (MVP) feature set
- Create your MVP prototype
- Test your MVP

An entrepreneur can gain the attention of investors very quickly if the product-market fit is made readily visible, easy to comprehend, and that fit is effectively reinforced. This makes things easy for everyone, and is the essence of a successful fundraising presentation.

No one wants to do things the hard way, and this certainly applies to an entrepreneur seeking funding. Simplify the process – analyze your startup through the lens of a potential investor:

- High-credibility management team. Most investors are more concerned about the people they are working with than the business idea itself. Experienced investors look for a well-rounded team. They want to see a team that will stay intact in the long run, is self-sufficient, and possesses the resourcefulness required to make the startup a success.

- The promise of growth potential. The potential upside is the biggest adrenaline trigger for investors. It's what gives them a "kick." One of the best ways to demonstrate growth potential is to build traction at the earliest opportunity. This is a great validation that there is a solid product-market fit and the possibility of scale-up when funding is in place. Mix that with a realistic forecast and you have a winner, as the investor sees it.

- Ease of scaling up. A business with an attractive MVP and paying customers is a great start! However, the business has to be scalable without complications. Factors like the need for a large workforce or extra-long sales cycles impede the scaling-up process. Think of companies like Facebook, Uber, or Alibaba. Consider the structure that allows Facebook to scale up as a media owner when it creates no content. A similar structure allows Uber to run a worldwide cab service without owning a single cab. Alibaba can provide retail opportunities worldwide without having to stock an inventory.

As the name suggests, investment banking deals with investments. Investment banks help individuals and organizations raise capital, and provide financial consultancy. They act as an intermediary between security issuers and investors. (Security issuers work on the availability of securities—shares, bonds, and warrants.)

THE DIFFERENCE BETWEEN
VENTURE CAPITALISTS AND ANGEL INVESTORS

Angel investors and venture capitalists (VCs) are, in the big picture, the same thing. However, there are some broad distinctions which can be drawn based upon the following questions:

- Who does the money invested belong to?
- How much money is to be invested?
- What is the contribution of the investor on the board?

Angel investors are generally high-net worth individuals on the lookout for promising startups in an early stage.

With an angel investor, the investment is made in an individual capacity or through a family office. The investment ticket in these cases tends to be smaller. This works in favor of early startups, which are generally looking for smaller monetary amounts to shape up the initial business idea. Angel investors tend to be interested in those startups about to launch or go to market.

The investments from angels come from their personal comfort. This means there can be faster decisions, shorter due diligence, and simpler shareholder agreements. Angels will generally not have a board seat. They expect around tenfold returns in three to five years.

> VCs, on the other hand, are a professional team of investors who bring funds from corporate entities, institutions, investors in the early stage, and high-growth companies.

The VCs themselves do not own the funding. VCs are interested in the equity of early-stage, high-growth small and medium enterprises. Their expertise lies in making the right startup investments that will bring exponential returns. They prefer large tickets ($2–3 million) and are interested in companies that have already launched and gained traction. This method of funding is aimed at rapid growth and expansion with huge investments in marketing, infrastructure, or manpower.

Unlike angel investors, VCs have a larger responsibility toward the stakeholders. The process of due diligence is tough and exhaustive, and managed by a group of people. VCs are also known to take significant control over the business and closely monitor business affairs, by having a seat on the board.

VCs generally expect a tenfold (or 30%) annual return and have a five-year exit plan. These numbers may depend on many factors such as growth and involvement.

RISK/REWARD PROFILE**

The risk of testing and running a startup profitably rests with the entrepreneur, but what is important to the investor is the risk/reward profile of that startup. The majority of new startups do not make it, so these risky investments often lead to bitter outcomes. The startups that do make it, however, will bring in rewards—and those are the ones investors are after.

That brings us to the risk/reward ratio. The question at stake is, how much prospective reward can an investor earn for every dollar they risk on an investment? The better the

> *A universal appeal for investors is the minimum ratio of two to one. You gain an investor's attention when they see the potential of at least doubling their money. Basically, it's the risk of losing $50 to make $100.*

ratio of risk to reward, the greater the appeal to the investor.

Innovative ideas need execution and funds. The entrepreneur must determine where to properly access the funds for their startup. A startup can be categorized in 4 types of funding:

- Self-funding
- Seed Capital
- Venture
- IPO

▸ **Self-funding:** The entrepreneur utilizes their own savings, funds, or resources to invest in their startup. This includes financial support extended from friends and family. The self-funding stage has fewer complexities and requires minimal documentation. Investments are sourced at much cheaper rates. Self-funding (or bootstrapping) is the preferred mode where small investment is required.

▸ **Seed capital:** This investment is made at an early stage. The business is in a preliminary phase of learning the customers and their preferences and tastes, in order to formulate a product or service based on its study of the market.

▶ **Venture:** This source of funding comes in when products or services have already reached the market. Any business or startup can pursue venture funding without regard to the profitability of its products. This stage can include multiple rounds of funding.

▶ **Series A:** In many cases this is the first round of funding. At this stage, the startup has already formulated a specific plan for its product or service. The fund is typically utilized for marketing and brand credibility. This may include tapping into new markets and gaining business growth.

▶ **Series B:** The series B fund is used for a business which is already established, which has marketing already set up correctly, and where customers are buying the product or service. The funding, in this case, helps to improve infrastructure, pay salaries, and hire competitive staff, in order to make the business a stronger player in the market.

▶ **Series C:** Series C can represent multiple investment rounds—there is no restriction on the number of funding rounds. The catch is that more rounds of investments means relinquishing more business equity.

▶ **Initial public offering (IPO):** This involves raising funds from the general public, including institutional investors, by selling the company's shares. When trying to establish an IPO, companies have to abide by applicable regulations. The funds are mostly used for further growth and diversification of business.

WHAT TYPES OF FUNDING SOURCES ARE OUT THERE?

The biggest mistake for any startup to avoid is approaching the wrong funding source. Unfortunately, entrepreneurs typically select the hardest resource to raise money. These include institutional equity-like capital firms, private equity firms, and corporations.

So what are the options? Let's look at them in detail. Before we do that, we have to understand the difference between equity financing and debt financing.

> *Equity financing means to exchange a portion of ownership of the business for financial investment.*

With an ownership stake in the company, an investor shares in the company profits. Equity is a permanent investment, and is not repaid by the company at a later date.

The parties who lend the funds are called creditors, and they earn from the interest paid by the borrower.

These are the chief funding sources available to startups:

> *Debt financing occurs when you borrow funds with the stipulation of paying back those funds with interest at a future date.*

▸ **Self-funding:** Many startups prefer to fund themselves. Doing this allows the startup to better focus on setting up the business from day one. This not only helps keep finances in check, but also allows the company to make decisions with full freedom. Sources include money from spouses, parents, family, or friends.

▸ **Crowdfunding:** Crowdfunding is made up of small amounts of capital contributed by a large number of individuals. This source of funds is accessed through vast networks of people on social media and crowdfunding websites. These platforms potentially open up a pool of investors beyond the traditional reach of owners, friends, relatives, and other funding sources.

▸ **Creative funding:** Creative funding involves taking a look at possibilities in order to tap into additional resources that you might otherwise have overlooked. This may include taking steps to cut corners and reduce unwanted expenses. It may also include investing money over time on your business, or devoting your weekends to it before quitting your day job. There are other options, which may include finding accommodating vendors (who may share your initial financial strain or get paid on a certain date every month). To find these resources, take a look at microloans or special programs. You might even use a credit card to fund an immediate hurdle.

▸ **Social or P2P lending:** You might want to consider

getting loans directly from other individuals. This eliminates the middleman, and accesses funds directly contributed by other individuals. Social lending websites bring borrowers and investors together to establish necessary rates and terms. These individual investors are mostly interested in an alternative to traditional banks to provide cash savings and better rates of interest.

▶ **Financial manoeuvring:** Consider taking some financial manoeuvres to bring in funding. Think about options like refinancing your mortgage, or driving a second-hand car instead of one that calls for a hefty monthly payment. This could free up a lot of money. Try to aggressively pursue a tax-advantaged investing strategy, like employee-sponsored 401(k)s and 403(b)s, IRAs, Roth IRAs, or other tax-advantaged accounts. You have options to cohabitate or marry. This suggestion might have some complications, but if you live with roommates or a long-term partner you can end up with substantial savings, including tax breaks. If you have a day job—how about seeking a new job with a better employer? Or moving somewhere cheaper?

▶ **Bank lines and loans:** Bank lines and loans offer you short-term, mid-term, or long-term financing. If you generate enough revenue to repay bank loans, this option becomes very attractive. It is worth mentioning: Banks offer flexible loan repayment options, and are willing to give you a contract that suits your needs.

▶ **Strategic financing:** The use of strategic financing involves long-term financial planning within the business. The objective of financial management is to maximize returns or shareholder wealth. This involves a long-term course of action around aspects of business management. (Examples: marketing and sales plan, production plan, personal plan, capital expenditure, and so forth.)

▸ **Grants:** Looking for free money to fund the startup? Consider getting grants. It could help you take care of paying salaries, buying stocks, or even reaching new customers. Grants are "free" in the sense that you don't have to pay them back. However, they are not handouts. You can't just shoot an email with the subject line "$$$ business grant please" and automatically get one. You need to apply for a grant, and it may take some decent work and effort on your part. Also – not everyone who applies gets a grant.

▸ **Lease:** You can use your tangible assets to bring in income without using debt or equity financing. The lease is a legal agreement between two parties that specifies the terms and conditions for rental use. When the lease ends, the asset is returned to the owner. The lease can be renewed or purchased, depending on what suits both the parties after the lease is over.

▸ **Individual equity:** When an individual invests in your company in return for a share of ownership, this is referred to as individual equity. When you access individual equity, investors become your partners, and expect a return on their investment. In addition to capital, individual equity investors also bring experience, connections, and know-how that will contribute to business growth. In many cases, entrepreneurs find a capable mentor who will also invest in their company.

▸ **Institutional equity:** When capital firms, private equity firms, and corporations invest in a business, they have what's referred to as institutional equity. These firms invest in a business based on the prospects of the company and anticipation of a future exit event that provides acceptable returns.

WHICH SOURCE OF FUNDS IS BEST FOR YOU?

With so many choices, the question of what source of funds to use may or may not have an obvious answer. You might wonder whether you should go with outside funding or bootstrap your business. Maybe you can do it with savings or ask your spouse for a contribution. If you do go for outside funding, which type should you go for? Most businesses in the initial stages are financed by home equity or private savings. Attracting outside equity at the start is a remarkable (and unlikely) feat. You have to take a serious look at your financial position, and be honest with yourself. That's all you need to do in order to take your best step forward. Once you are in the thick of things, you will have a better handle on what your best investments can be, and how much you should target for additional or external funding. You have a great responsibility as founder of your company. You are its heart and soul. You are passionate about the business and committed to its goals. But your larger responsibility is all about leadership.

As a leader, you must mobilize your team and keep them motivated to deliver. You might have expertise in a certain skill like product development, marketing, sales, or technology, but you must evolve as a leader of the business as a whole, united entity. A full-time founder/CEO generates more confidence in investors. Most startup businesses are demanding, and a leader who wants to succeed can't be just part-time, especially when it is time to seek investors.

So what is a founder/CEO expected to do? I warn you, not everything on this list may appeal to you. However, these eleven tasks will constitute a major part of your day-to-day role.

▶ **Manage the board of directors:** The board of directors may contribute immensely, but most of the time they are a major distraction for young startups. It's up to you as a CEO/founder/co-founder to handle the board in a manner that keeps them focused on the goal. You have to decide what type of board the company should have, who should be on it, and even how it operates.

▶ **Create the vision:** Creation of value for customers is the top priority for any founder. You have to create and continuously evolve a powerful, simple, and unique vision. This is your best chance to bring in commitment from internal and external stakeholders toward the goals you have set. A powerful vision enables everyone to stick to the common goals along the path of the startup journey.

▶ **Find and retain the best talent:** Finding the right talent is a big challenge for any startup. A good core team is a step in the right direction. Serial entrepreneurs tend to gain more attention than first-time entrepreneurs (even if they failed in earlier ventures). A founder has to go that extra mile to acquire the best talent available. You might need to figure out where you can utilize freelancers or remote workers. You have to keep the fine balance between quality, productivity, and cost. It is vital for you to keep creating immense value for your customers.

▶ **Form and lead the executive team:** You need an action-oriented executive team, and you have to lead it yourself. This is critical, because your business operations will ultimately contribute to your startup's success on the ground.

▶ **Empower and delegate:** As the founder, you are in a unique position to see the big picture across your team's roles and skill sets, the markets, and your customer base. This gives you an unfair advantage. But you can't be better than your team. How will you use this as leverage to empower your team? You have to ask yourself questions like: What can I do to equip my team better so they make better decisions? This question needs an answer which utilizes a context only you can provide.

▶ **As a founder,** you have to ensure that you don't make more than 10% of the total key decisions. If you do, it means you have already failed in some way. You may have missed filling a role, hired a wrong person, lack context, or you have not clearly defined areas of responsibility. Maybe you have simply not empowered your team to make decisions.

▶ **Prioritize and set KPIs:** Founders find themselves knee-deep in the various responsibilities of running a business. These may not all be immediate priorities. To keep your business on track, it's important to track the right KPIs and work on a priority set of genuine business needs.

▸ **Raise funds:** Raising funds requires a lot of homework, and the burden is on you to identify the right investors for your business. As a founder, you should be in sync with the investment market in your industry all the time. It is important to be in contact with the right people in the right networks who can lead you to a potential investor.

▸ **Make a business plan:** You might want someone to assist you with business planning. This is a vital aspect of your business that, as a founder, you cannot overlook. An early-stage startup relies heavily on its business plan for the day-to-day activities, so it has to be closely supervised all the time.

▸ **Manage and plan finances:** Until you get a dedicated CFO, the responsibility to manage the finances is on you. The founder needs to have a handle on how much money the business is spending to run the operation, versus the need for funding. This is especially important when the startup is growing at a rapid pace.

▸ **Engage your team:** As a founder, you are expected to keep your team cohesive and engaged all the time. You must avoid favoritism and bias while at the same time being supportive and approachable. You cannot be right all the time. Your team should be able to think freely and focus on context. Running a startup is an extremely enriching experience for the founder and team members. Be open to considering a co-founder when your limits are challenged. Expanding your team with the right people at the right time is a major force in the success of your startup.

HOW SHOULD YOU APPROACH AND CLOSE ROUNDS FOR FUNDING?

Before you talk to anyone about funding your startup, you need a clear picture of what you want to do, how to do it, what costs it will incur, and the profits it will generate. You also need to be able to ensure you that you garner people's (investors') attention, and communicate your vision smoothly and confidently. The better you are prepared, the better your chance to have a meaningful discussion.

Preparation is the key. You will need to have a set of tools that will enable you to effectively present your vision to potential investors. Those tools are:

- The business plan
- The elevator pitch
- The pitch deck

As we discuss these items, you will see that these tools work together. The full details of your startup are contained in the business plan. You will identify and use the key points from your business plan when you have the opportunity to deliver an elevator pitch. When you deliver a more complete presentation to potential investors, you will use a pitch deck to get across the big picture without all of the details.

The exciting and fulfilling conclusion to the successful pitch deck presentation is – a request for your business plan. This is where your hard work really pays off.

If you have your tools ready, you have maximized your chances of successfully acquiring funding that can propel your startup.

Just relax and enjoy – this part can be a lot of fun!

2

THE FUNDRAISING TOOLS

 ## THE BUSINESS PLAN

A business plan is a prerequisite to raise capital. It's also a great practice for the management of your business. When you seek funding, the business plan accomplishes several things for entrepreneurs, the most important being – it establishes that you have thought your idea through carefully. It also establishes financial benchmarks to which you then hold yourself accountable. Investors want to see well thought-out numbers, along with where and how

> A business plan helps you justify the amount of funding you are requesting and the reasons why.

the money is allocated, to achieve the best results. It's important to maintain your credibility since you never know which other doors your pitch might open next. As you grow, you may need additional rounds of funding.

Developing a business plan allows you to deep-dive into realistic assumptions. Many startups don't survive through the planning stage because they don't take this reflective step to determine what their startup can be expected to accomplish.

Your business plan should make economic sense, for sure. But it should also be something that you will dedicate yourself to passionately. The plan should be something you want to update and revisit as your company grows. The business plan is not a tool to write and then throw in a drawer. Check it often – it is your roadmap to a successful operation.

The business plan structures your interactions with investors and helps you get into meaningful discussions.

How difficult is it to write a business plan? Many will say it's a daunting task. But let me tell you – it is much easier than you think. Why? For the most part, business plans follow a boilerplate format. Your potential investors want to see specific details about your business, and in a certain order. It's fairly easy to cover all those predetermined points in detail, and by the way – get to know them by heart. You are now developing information that will be vital when you get a chance to do an elevator pitch or pitch deck presentation. Learn the details well. Trust me, taking the time to do this will serve you well. If you get an unexpected question during a presentation, you want to be ready with an answer.

There are various templates available online to develop your business plan, but the following four sections definitely need to be included:

Executive summary:

The executive summary is very much like your elevator pitch. It is a recap of all that is covered in your business plan. Since it is the first section in your business plan, it gets a lot of attention. A good executive summary "hooks" the reader, making them inclined to learn more about the business.

Most executive summaries cover:

- A short description of the business and a unique solution to the customer problem/
- A paragraph about marketing that includes the size of the market, sales forecast, the demography of potential customers, competition, and any competitive advantages/
- A paragraph about management, leadership, and industry experience, operation/staffing/location, and management dispositions/
- A financial section, maybe a long paragraph, about projected income and cash generated in the first three years; if you are seeking funding, this paragraph should also include the exact amount requested and how you plan to use it/

Although it may seem counterintuitive, it's recommended that you write your executive summary after you have your business plan ready. A business plan has to be developed from the bottom upward.

Marketing plan:

Finding customers is the top priority for any startup. Business managers spend considerable time to develop a marketing plan and then execute it. A marketing plan helps your business generate demand, which in turn results in sales.

The marketing plan has three main sections: market analysis, competitive analysis, and a marketing action plan.

Market Analysis:

There are two important aspects of market analysis:

- Figure out the market size and its potential. This helps investors understand whether there are sufficient buyers in the market to generate satisfactory revenue.

- Describe your ideal customer profile so they can be reached effectively through an outreach program.

Competitive Analysis:

This section ascertains the competition your startup faces in the marketplace. Ideally, list at least five competitors, along with their strengths and weaknesses, which may be issues like accessibility, pricing, return policy, reputation, marketing budget size, terms of service, complementary services, buying quantities, or associated costs.

Marketing Action Plan:

Marketing action planning is about driving traffic to your sales counter. What will you do to ensure a steady pipeline of customers who purchase your product?

The marketing action plan includes a step-by-step approach to attract customers. The total cost of carrying out this plan will be the marketing budget.

Specify whether you will be executing this action plan on your own, or seeking assistance. Lay out your sales expectations, which will become your sales forecast.

Key management:

Most of the time the startup founder gains entry into uncharted territory by setting up on their own. They have a limited track record and assets to take on the journey. Anyone who joins the startup in any way, including by making investments, is betting on it.

- The credibility of the startup is not limited to the founder. Key people working with him also add to the credibility of the startup to become a success. Demonstrate both the technical and leadership skills of key management, along with their operational expertise.

- Key management is represented in the form of short bios that complement the need that each person fills. If there are any experience or skill gaps, how do you plan to address them? You need to address that, most logically by indicating that you will bring other people onto the team.

Financial plan:

The financial plan vets the overall viability of the enterprise. Financial statements are oriented around charts and numbers. This section clearly states the assumptions for the financial projections, and how the whole enterprise is supposed to make a profit.

Many entrepreneurs dread this section, and their anxiety results in a massive holdup. Completion of the business plan is delayed while the entrepreneur procrastinates due to an inadequate understanding of the numbers and constraints.

Start with an introductory page that lays down

everything in plain English, and which will include the assumptions made, and how they were determined. Make reasonable assumptions, so that readers find the financial statements credible.

You must justify the sections about marketing planning and strategy with good numbers and solid bottom line projections. Whether you go for external funding or not, this section will help you steer your business successfully.

The financial plan also tells you whether the business is viable, or will be a waste of time and money. You may even reconsider going to market with this idea in the first place. Better to stop before committing funds, time and talent on an unproductive idea, than pursue an option that readily appears to be unviable. It's extremely important to get this section right, so you know clearly where your idea stands!

Here are some salient points in preparing the financial plan:

- The financial statement is not accounting. Financial projections do include balance sheets, profit and loss, cash flow, and so forth, but that does not mean it's accounting. Remember, accounting takes the historical view, looking back in time from 'today'. The financial statement is about looking into the future starting from 'today'.

- The financial plan is an elaborate "educated guess"-it is not tax reporting. It's more about summarizing and aggregation than accounting.

- The rule of thumb in financial planning is: be realistic. Find a balance and avoid being too optimistic or pessimistic.

- Investors, including your family and friends, want to see

numbers that reasonably indicate potential for profits, and a clearly defined exit strategy.

■ The financial forecast includes things like a sales forecast, expenses budget, cash flow statement, income projections, dealing with assets and liabilities, and breakeven analysis.

■ "Plans are useless, but planning is essential." Use the plans frequently for planning. Don't just look at them once a year. Update your plans regularly with the new information you have gathered from being in an actual operating mode. Plans are supposed to help you manage your business better, help you revise estimates, and keep your projections realistic.

■ Use pictorial charts, not just in financial planning but in other sections of your business plan too. Most investors like to see visuals.

So, there you go. No business plan is complete without the key elements mentioned above.

> *The executive summary, marketing plan, key management bios, and financial planning sections are the foundation of business planning.*

You might include additional sections as needed. Maybe you want to adapt your business plan to a specific purpose or audience.

The first priority of the business plan is the executive summary. It's the introduction and the "hook," which will engage your readers, and make them interested in knowing more about your idea. Miss that part, and you risk losing the game.

 **THE ELEVATOR PITCH**

The elevator pitch is a short, persuasive speech about your business. It needs to explain your business concept, and how it creates value for its customers. Keep it short and sweet, so you can use it on a short elevator ride (hence the name). Keep this pitch between thirty seconds and two minutes.

> *The main focus of an elevator pitch is to keep it concise and direct.*

The first two sentences are the "hook" – they are really important and should gain the listener's attention. It's a good idea to use simple language and avoid unnecessary details. Don't get bogged down in trying to explain your whole business model. Remember, the elevator is moving!

You will have to adjust the pitch based on the identity of your listener. Continuously refine it as your organization grows. Remain flexible and adaptable while you deliver the pitch. It should flow genuinely and fluently, without giving the impression that it's scripted.

The elevator pitch is a great tool to present your business in very short or introductory meetings. The pitch can get people interested in your idea and potentially secure you some meetings with investors or stakeholders in no time.

The potential investors you are approaching are busy people. Treat them with respect. Don't just rush up and jump into your pitch. You might open with "Do you have a minute? I have an idea I'd like to tell you about." If the person says they don't have time right now, but specifies when you can talk later – that's a big win! You've shown professionalism by your approach, and respect for their time. The result – you now have a commitment to a short meeting to present your business concept.

Here are some simple steps to consider as you create a great elevator pitch. It may take some time for you to get it right, but this is a short meeting that can determine the future of your company, so spend some time to get the right flow and content. Vary your approach until you arrive at a presentation that's compelling, and sounds natural in conversation.

- What's your goal? What is the objective of your pitch? Do you want to tell someone about your business for future collaboration? Or do you want to secure a meeting with this investor you just met? Your goal will direct your presentation, so determine – for each situation – your goal, before you make the approach. Otherwise, you will risk appearing unprepared or off topic for that listener. What do you do? Focus on the problems you solve, the value you bring, and how your product or service changes the situation for your customers. Don't shy away from using numbers, but don't make it complicated.

■ Put an effort into what you want your audience to remember, and then use your pitch and style of delivery to make a lasting impact. Can your pitch bring a smile and signal a great opportunity? Add a bit of enthusiasm and confidence, and you are well on the right path.

■ Do you clearly communicate your unique selling proposition (USP)? This is the single element that makes you memorable. A quick mention of USP is a great addition—immediately after you explain what you do.

■ Get the listener talking. When it looks like they want to speak – know when to stop talking. You can very easily kill a pitch by overtalking. The idea is to quickly engage with your audience, rather than simply walking away after you deliver the pitch. Ask some open-ended questions and strike up a conversation. Answer questions if any are posed, and patiently listen in case your audience opens up. Their response could be a signal that you will land a more planned discussion at a later time. Bring it together. When you have each section of the elevator pitch ready, put it all together. Read it aloud and rehearse it multiple times. Keep rounding out the parts that seem out of place and make it short and sweet. Time yourself, and aim for thirty seconds. Make it as snappy and compelling as possible. A well-rehearsed thirty-second pitch can always be improved (and perhaps lengthened) impromptu, as needed. This is where your familiarity with the details about your company can come in really handy. If you have those answers readily available, you'll be well prepared for any question that comes up.

- Practice makes the pitch perfect. It will help you gain the right tempo, and give you good control over your words and body language. When you train yourself properly, you will deliver the elevator pitch naturally. It will come off as a smooth conversation, without being aggressive or salesy. You've got to be succinct while conveying all the important information. It's highly recommended that you practice your pitch in front of the mirror, or for friends and colleagues.

It's a thoughtful touch to hand over a small takeaway after your pitch, like a brochure or one-page graphic representation of your business, or at the very least your business card.

> *A pitch deck is a brief presentation to provide your audience with a quick overview of your business plan.*

Preparing for the Presentation

A pitch deck is prepared using presentation software like PowerPoint, Keynote, or Prezi. When you pitch using such a presentation, always try to tell a story and engage with people emotionally. There has to be a human feel to it. How about starting with a quick story about your startup?

Keep things short and sweet—if you use anything more than ten slides, you challenge the constraints of time and attention span. Avoid crowding the slides with too much information or too many bullet points. Try to limit the content to one idea per slide, so you have everyone on the same page. Don't present the content on the slide word for word in a flat voice— emphasize your tone and technique. Maintain eye contact and continually feel out the audience. Keep in mind that the first two to three minutes are the crucial first impression.

Work on consistency, and follow your brand guidelines. This includes using the same font, size, color, and capitalization formats. Keep your presentation high on visuals and low on text. Visuals go a long way to grab attention and emotionally engage the audience.

Last but not least, know your metrics by heart. It tells a lot about your passion and commitment to your concept.

Focus on things your team members have accomplished, and how they bring a wealth of experience to the table which will help make your business a success.

- **Introduction:** Who you are and what you do. Again, short and sweet.

- **Your team:** The people behind the idea and their roles.

- **The problem:** What problem does your business solve. Your USP. The thing that's different about the way you do it and how.

- **Your solution:** How you solve the problem and what you will change.

- **Your product or service:** How your product or service works. Demonstrate with examples.

- **Market potential:** Whether the traction is measurable, and how many customers you must serve to prove your market potential.

- **Market share:** The size of your target market.

- **Competition:** What your competitors are doing, and how you provide alternative solutions to the same problems they solve.

- **Business model:** How you make money. Do you have a schedule with projections?

- **Investing:** Your budget and the amount of investment you're looking to acquire.

- **Contact:** The best way to contact you.

Practice Your Pitch

Once you have your business plan ready, the next obvious step is to pitch it to the prospects. It's important to practice first, because even if you have a good business plan, pitching it correctly will make all the difference. Investors do not invest in your planning skills, but rather in you and the other people who are proposing the idea.

Before you practice your pitch, there are few primary things to sort out:

- Who is your target audience? Have a clear understanding of who this pitch is for. Do a little homework. If the pitch is for a specific investor, why not find out what their current investment portfolio looks like?

- Understand the general thought pattern of the investor. The first thing to establish is the "seriousness" of the problem and how you will solve it. The investor should be able to relate to the problem.

- Understand how many people are affected by that problem, and the potential traction that may be realized. How many people suffer from the "pain points" caused by the problem?

- If all the above is good (*A problem exists; *Good solution is proposed; *Enough potential customers exist), you should next determine how defensible the idea is. Can it be protected via patents, trademarks, etc.?

It is a sad fact that many entrepreneurs fail to prepare for their pitches. There might be different reasons for this, like thinking it's not important since the business plan is solid, or being overconfident, or very busy, or just not feeling like it.

But consider your situation: You are going to face an outsider who is interested in providing an investment in your business. If they are really interested – that's when they are most likely to get very critical, and want to see how successfully you can address the issues they raise. If you make your presentation with hardly any preparation, it can push you into uncharted waters. You're supposed to be ready and able to leverage every bit of your presentation.

A good way to prepare for presentation is to form an internal team of critics and do your presentation for them as a dry run. You could also enter a business planning competition in your local area. These low-risk environments can "stress test" and considerably enhance your presentation capabilities.

So there you have it! It's essential to have a credible business plan, but you must also present your case persuasively and with conviction.

> *"You gotta make me feel like I'm going to miss out."*
> – *Dragons' Den investor Simon Woodroffe*

Know Your Numbers

This can't be stressed enough: You should know your

numbers well. Don't fumble on obvious and minor details that are most likely to be raised. Ideally, start working on your pitch as soon as business planning commences. Business planning is not an excuse for you to hold off on creating the pitch deck and being prepared to present it. Many investors will read the executive summary and, if interested, immediately ask for a presentation to explain things in detail. A business plan might be read in entirety only after a successful presentation is delivered.

A typical investor has a great eye for detail. Use your pitch deck to reinforce the idea, and avoid raking up sloppy contradictions that don't match the proposal you intend to make.

Using presentation software like PowerPoint has inherent advantages, but don't get into analysis paralysis. Be careful about things like the maximum number of slides in your pitch deck (no more than ten to twelve). Rigorously analyze the relevance and clarity of each element you include on the slides.

Ensure that the investors receive a copy of the deck, which may contain more details than the version you presented (use appendices).

Be prepared to undertake a Q&A session. Answering questions presents a great opportunity to share more facts, and develop that positive reinforcement and rapport.

Learn from Mistakes

Do not get disheartened when you are unsuccessful with your pitch. Not everything is in your control. The investor and the investment are just like a job interview – sometimes it's just not a good fit. Many times you will have to let it go. But next time, think through the odds, and see what you can do to improve your position.

Take feedback seriously, and use it to continuously improve your pitch. Analyze the questions you receive and which part of the pitch they relate to. Do those questions point to a weakness in your business proposition that you can strengthen for your next pitch opportunity? Pitch the most important investor later rather than sooner, since you will learn a lot from your early pitch sessions.

Ideally, the purpose of the pitch should complement the questions that you receive. There is a tendency to get lost in details, and lose the attention of a potential investor in the process. Remember, the presentation is about funding. Ensure that the investor receives sufficient information to ask the right questions, but not a lot of unnecessary details that will redirect their focus from your main business proposition.

COMPLETING YOUR COMMUNICATION TOOLS FOR INVESTORS

Before we move ahead, let's summarize for a moment. By this point, we have discussed in length the importance of the executive summary, business planning, and financial strategy. Remember that it is important to take these steps long before the stage of identifying, targeting, and engaging with potential investors.

The fundraising process consists of several stages, and you first need your communication tools to be properly prepared, in order to successfully meet, communicate, and raise money from investors. These include, in the order you will typically need to present them:

- The elevator pitch
- The executive summary
- The pitch deck (presentation to investors)
- The business plan

These speeches and documents will help you convey the appropriate amount of information as you progress through the various stages of funding. As you move ahead, you will share increasingly detailed and confidential information with the investors as part of due diligence.

The first step is normally the elevator pitch and executive summary. Investors will evaluate the information provided, and decide whether they want to learn more about your business idea. If their decision is in the affirmative, they will generally ask for a presentation (your pitch deck). The business plan may be provided at the same time or soon afterward.

3

PART

GETTING THE RIGHT INVESTORS

To make an investment in a startup is risky, speculative, and can result in total loss. Investors carefully consider the potential risks associated with their investments. The following are the potential risks from their perspective (a bit of this list is repetitive, but worth it). It is important to look at the dynamic of pitching investors from the viewpoint of the investor, to better understand their perspective.

Investment Risks

- **Principal risk:** The entire amount of investment is at risk, particularly in scenarios where the company may fail, or the investor may not be able to sell their stocks.

- **Returns risk:** The returns on investment are highly variable and not guaranteed. Some startups might succeed and generate significant returns, while others may generate small or negligible returns. These returns may also vary in terms of frequency and time frame. Investing in a startup is not about the regular, predictable, or stable return.

- **Returns delay:** Returns can take several years to be realized. Many startups take five to seven years before they generate an investment return. It may take even longer before a startup produces any return at all.
- **Liquidity risk:** It's not easy to sell startup securities, since they are privately held companies. These stocks are not traded in the public stock exchange. There may also be restrictions on your ability to transfer or resell your securities.

Security Risks

- **Instrument risk:** Each type of security—preferred equity, common equity, or convertible notes—has different inherent risks.
- **Dilution:** When startup companies need additional capital, new investors receive newly issued securities. These securities further dilute the percentage ownership of previous investors.
- **Minority stake:** Smaller investors have lower voting rights and little ability to decide the direction of the company. Larger investors have an upper hand in protecting their interests in the company.
- **Valuation risk:** The value of private companies, particularly startups, is difficult to assess. The issuer may overprice the shares and you risk overpaying for your investment. The price you pay will have a material impact on your eventual return.

Business Risks

- **Failure risk:** A startup investment is speculative, because the startup may fail. The success of a startup depends on their new product or service, and their ability to find a market. These are tricky matters to navigate for a startup. Therefore, the investor has to be prepared to lose the entire investment.

■ **Revenue risk:** In the early stages, there is no assurance that the company will make a profit. Companies in the early stage of development have to tackle a myriad of issues before they reach the next stage. Unexpected business problems, difficulties, expenses, complications, and delays may inhibit the ability to make a profit.

■ **Funding risk:** Companies at the startup stage require more funds than they have existing cash resources. They have to manage operating expenses, product development, and administrative activities and expand marketing. A company may not receive additional funding when it is needed. The terms for funds to become available may be unfavorable. This could result in delays and even losses, potentially ceasing operations altogether.

■ **Disclosure risks:** A startup company may not be in a position to provide all the information about business plans and operations for various reasons. This may include a lack of understanding or immaturity in managing newly founded operations and trading. This has inherent risk, because the company is obligated to provide the investor limited information about business and financial matters.

■ **Fraud risks:** There is a possibility that people involved in the company may commit fraud or mislead investors. If this happens, the whole investment is at stake. It's the investors' responsibility to carry out necessary due diligence, to account for the possible occurrence of fraud.

- **Lack of professional guidance:** Early-stage startups may lack professional guidance. The early success of a company may be attributed to smaller investors who bring limited leverage in terms of resources, contacts, and experience in execution. A lack of reputable angel investors or venture capital firms in the current funding round can throw up unique challenges around developing a successful operation.

- **Growth risk:** Any startup has to grow significantly to succeed. There are no guarantees success will happen. There is no foolproof way to assess whether the current financial systems, procedures, and controls within the company will successfully expand as the company grows.

- **Competition risk:** The company may face competition from other companies with better leverage in terms of funding, expertise, or strategy. There may be a risk of a price war and one company losing out completely. This can cause a material effect on companies' operations and financial stability.

- **Market demand risk:** There is no assurance that products will be accepted in the market, even if they are able to fight competition and address other dynamics within the market.

- **Control risks:** Founders, directors, and executive officers hold a major stake in the business. The interests of investors and founders may diverge from each other, leading to a struggle for control of the company. In those situations, the founders of the company have greater influence over corporate actions. This can greatly limit companies' stock prices or even prevent investors from realizing the return on their investment.

Consider the following points to deve op a target list of investors:

■ **Match yourself with investors' "sweet spots."** Most investor groups have their own established set of investment criteria. To best utilize your time, it's important to understand each group's specialty or interest, so you can approach the one that best fits your opportunity. This might be typically be based on:

  ■ *Sector investment focus:* Most investment groups (angel or institutional investors) specialize in a particular sector like software, life sciences, cleantech, or communications. It's important to approach investors who specialize in your startup's business sector.

  ■ *Investment stage and fund size:* The stage at which investment is made (also called the "preferred stage of development") is another specialization of many investors. They generally prefer investing during specific stages in the development of a business. The same applies to the investment amount. Better to assess and reach out to investors who fund investments that best match the amount you need

Stage of Financing	Amount of Investment	Use of Proceeds
Seed	$50,000 - $500,000	– Develop a product – Prove that it works – Market research – Some initial IP work
Startup	$50,000– $1,000,000	– Marketing and production
Early stage	$500,000– $15,000,000	– Typically the company is still pre-revenue, but has completed a prototype
Later stage	$2,000,000– $15,000,000	– At this stage, companies usually have products, revenues, and other partnerships
Mezzanine stage	$2,000,000- $20,000,000	– Usually profitable, potential IPO or M&A candidate
Bridge	$2,000,000 - $20,000,000	– Funding is designed to bridge the company to an IPO within 3–12 months

Source: *Cardis, J. (2001). Venture Capital—The Definitive Guide for Entrepreneurs, Investors, and Practitioners. New York: John Wiley & Sons, Inc.*

- *Geography:* Most investors want to be 'hands on' with their investments and prefer to be able to visit the site of the business they invest in, with only a couple of hours of flight time.

- **Investor risk profile:** There is a considerable risk in early-stage investing, and investors prefer certain risk profiles over others. Following is a quick rundown of what this means.

Product Risk: Whether the product functions properly is an inherent risk—a common one for early-stage startups. This is particularly relevant in the case of new science or tech.

Market adoption risk: Will customers buy the product? Product/market fit is important. This is the risk of getting your first customers, gaining momentum, and the challenges surrounding value proposition and pricing.

Market size risk: Most companies flatten out on revenue once they reach a certain stage. Software companies. for example, will flatten out at a revenue of around $15–25 million. Even if they don't, it's extremely difficult to reach beyond the $100 million mark. This is ultimately a market-size question—and the inherent risk.

Market timing risk: A good product is a one which meets a need or solves a problem for today. If you enter into the market early or late, you tend to face the risk of an unfavorable market timing. IoT (Internet of things), for example, may not be early at the moment, but a product around that tech invites assessment.

Competitive risk: How many players are in the market? This may be a good or bad thing depending on the interests of an investor. A harder question to answer: Is the market a suitable place to enter as a new startup when dominant players already exist, and there are a dozen other competing startups?

Financing risk: How much capital is needed before the business succeeds? Depending on the sector and maturity of the market, the necessary funds can be really large, which presents a daunting prospect for investors. A company in cleantech or biotech, for example, might require hundreds of millions of dollars. This might be a situation where investors just don't want to face that level of financial risk.

Execution risk: A business may rely on a specific execution approach which might be hard to accomplish. For instance, running a global business on drone-based delivery has a lot of inherent risks that won't be attractive to investors. Management team risk: How well-equipped is the management team to accomplish the set goals? Are there any specific key roles still unfilled? VCs are ultimately investing in people, and gaps in the expertise of the team pose a risk.

Exit risk: Healthy revenue and margins are good, but the business should be able to grow, in order to provide substantial ROI. Good business in some niche markets may not be strategic or may be too small for public markets. This may hinder the exit strategy of the investor.

- Targeting the right investors. Now it's time to summarize investor profiles and identify the right firms. Here's how:

  - Websites: Look for investor associations and local chapters that list investors or member firms. Identify a few and go to their websites. Review their investment criteria and understand whether they are a good match for your opportunity.

- Word of mouth: Use your network, talk with peers, and discuss firms that are actively investing in your space.

- Industry conferences: Participants in industry conferences include a good number of investors. If you attend, you may be able to network with some good investor possibilities.

- News and trends in mass media publication: Keep abreast of the financing news in your sector. Are you subscribed to leading newsletters and magazines? You can't afford to miss important updates related to funding in your space.

Based on the information you gather, target a minimum of ten investors. Develop a tracking list to monitor your progress as you begin to contact these investors. Develop clarity around how you will stage your future interactions with each investor. You may also include other sources of financing on this list, like government programs or debt financing.

Let's get into some "don'ts" on ways to successfully acquire investors. You might think that it's unlikely to find yourself working with a wrong investor or even that there is such a thing as one. However, this is considered a major risk, and is more common than you would imagine. The consequences to your startup from connecting with an investor that doesn't fit your needs can be devastating, so choose carefully.

Don't pick investors who are infatuated with your idea. You might wonder, why in the world would you step away from an investor who really loves your idea? If you decide to pivot and kill the idea, this investor is likely to make your life difficult, simply because they have such an emotional investment in the idea. There can be many reasons you might change your mind about your original idea. You may get a better idea, or the market is not ready for your original concept, or you can't realistically scale up, or maybe you are risking a burnout by trying to pursue your original concept. It can then get complicated, because your investor doesn't want to cut losses and move on – he wants to continue with the idea, and can push uncomfortably hard to continue.

You want a team, including investors, which can survive difficult and demanding times, in order to validate ideas and then adapt to market needs quickly. This gives both parties enough room to pivot if a change is needed. You

> *The best investors will count on your team more than the idea, as they understand that success comes from a great team and its combined skills and passion.*

should also avoid investors who want to be a "friend." Remember time is money; you are looking for investments, not company for dinners and drinks. You can always find better ways to spend that time. The status of being an investor is thrilling, and invites flattery and stardom. Many 'wannabes' are attracted to this compelling position. Keep in mind that a wealthy person with cash at their fingertips is different from a professional startup investor. 'Wannabe' investors can quickly become a liability and add to your stress. Be selective and accept funding only from investors with a proven and successful track record.

3

 **CONTACTING FUNDING SOURCES**

Now you are all set to reach out. It's time to get out there, meet the right people, and discuss great opportunities.

Resist the temptation to shoot your executive summary to investors via email. Investors give almost zero attention to this method of approach. The best way to meet them is always through a referral, or face-to-face meeting at a networking event. Having an established connection is extremely important, and when you can strike up a conversation in this manner, it's natural and spontaneous. You will have to continuously keep track of where your investors are seen, and which upcoming event is likely to attract their attendance. Once you manage to strike up a conversation with them, use your elevator pitch.

At this stage, clearly outline your "call to action" for that person—which could be a meeting, an introduction, or an opportunity to touch base over time. If the investor engages, be ready to expand the discussion. If it feels appropriate, offer them a printout of your executive summary, schedule a presentation, or both.

There are various ways to get positively noticed by

investors. This may include accepting speaking engagements, entering pitching competitions, or even attending industry conferences. It's best to avoid cold calling, but you can always reach out to investors by asking for a time to meet. If you do get an opportunity this way, maximize it. Once you have a list of at least mildly interested investors, reach out to them via a concise, well-crafted email. You can introduce yourself and your company, and let them know about your business.

In most cases, if your email catches their attention, they will research you and your business online. Expect this step, because that's what the successful investor – who you want to work with – will do. It is part of their due diligence. You can gain great leverage here if you are already active on the web. Your name and business name searches are often the first things many investors will see. Therefore your search results, along with content like press mentions, customer reviews, and even activity on Facebook, LinkedIn, or Twitter can turn things in your favor.

If an investor gets interested in you, they will request more information from you than is available online. If they ask you for specific items like an executive summary, business plan, or team profile, give them just that. Don't flood them with materials they did not ask for.

Getting to investors involves passing through "pit stops" of sorts many times over. Ultimately the real progress is when you get a request for an in-person pitch. The in-person pitch is one of the most crucial moments in this journey. It is a very short period of time where you have to accomplish a lot, so be well prepared. You have to keep your pitch concise and straight to the point. Leave plenty of time for investors' questions and discussions afterward.

If the pitch extends into a lengthy discussion where they want to learn more about your concept and your business – congratulations! That's a huge expression of interest, and could lead to a successful investment in your company! It's a wonderful feeling to walk out of a 10-minute pitch session and realize that it lasted over an hour.

PITCHING YOUR DEAL TO FUNDING SOURCES

Earlier, we discussed how to create your pitch deck. Now let's talk about how to deliver it.

Pitching your deal to an investor is the moment of truth. This is what you have been waiting for. Think of all the work you did to get here. Relax, and be confident and professional!

Here are some points to keep in mind.

- **Be brief and to the point:** Professional investors are known for short attention spans and are always under pressure to make decisions quickly. This is not the time to be long-winded. Use the lingo. The more you talk in the language of investing, the easier your investors will understand you. Talking in terms familiar to them makes it easy to focus the conversation effectively, where investors will be able to ask the right questions, and you are in a better position to clarify your statements. Avoid abstractions and talk in specifics. Try to steer clear of industry buzzwords and tech-speak.

- **Do talk about risks:** Hiding the risk in the business is an absolute no-no. Investors are very aware that every business has associated risks. Hiding risk is a poor way to kick off a business relationship. It always helps to be open about the inherent risk in your concept, then anticipate potential weaknesses in the business idea that investors might notice.

- **Don't just stop after sharing those risks:** Detail your plan of risk mitigation, and demonstrate how you plan to overcome those issues. This transparency assures investors and gives them confidence to take the relationship to the next level. They'll see you as a problem solver, and someone who can deal with unforeseen challenges that will arise.

- **Do include the exit strategy:** As you look for capital, investors are looking for returns and exit strategies. It's a good idea to include a clear and realistic exit plan. Underline how the investments shall be rewarded, ranging from interest and profits from the sale, to an IPO.

- **Be clear about what happens next:** After you have described the details about your company, tell investors what you want from them, as well as what you are going to do with the funds they provide once they are received. Be clear about the amount you seek, the terms you offer, and how the capital will be utilized.

- **Listen:** Don't get carried away with your agenda. Be ready to listen, and be open to feedback. When investors begin talking, it's a good sign. Answer all their questions thoroughly and thoughtfully. Don't get defensive or interpret their questions as attacks on your idea or business plan. Their questions indicate that they are interested in the opportunity you have presented. This is exactly what you want!

- **Learn:** Investors are experienced professionals and can glean an accurate impression of the aspects of your business that could make them successful. Even if your interaction doesn't lead to funding, the experience it will bring is worth it. You will learn a lot about what investors look for, and how you can enhance your pitch or bring improvements to your business concept.

- **Inspire confidence:** Being confident is important in any presentation. In the early stage of funding, your presentation is more about selling yourself than your business. Investors look for confident leaders who inspire confidence, and are ready to tackle real-life challenges. However, there is a thin line between confidence and arrogance. You don't have to be arrogant.

- **Keep the business plan in focus:** Everything you have done so far leads to the presentation of your business plan. The slew of emails, research, and presentations will get your feet in the door. But what clinches the deal is a thorough, meticulous business plan. You cannot talk investors into investing. They will do their due diligence on your business plan. When you finally hand over your detailed business plan, ensure that it is the best possible representation of your business.

- **Get investors excited:** The goal of your in-person pitch is to present a business opportunity that is too good to pass up. Bring in powerful ideas and undeniable data, along with confidence and creativity, and investors will be compelled to give you their attention.

- **Be persistent:** Pitching to investors is a marathon, not a sprint. You may have to pitch a dozen times to the same investor before you get funded. You will also find yourself in between various stages with different investors. Some will confirm presentation dates but then cancel on you. Some will never follow up after the first meeting. Others may seem like they are almost convinced but may appear to drag their feet endlessly. You have to be persistent and play the game with patience.

■ **Practice:** This is what will make the pitch perfect. Regardless of what happens with a particular investor, keep learning. Identify areas that need improvement, or make any changes that are deemed fit. You will keep discovering things that will make you faster, smarter, and better, which will allow you to locate the weak points in your pitches and eliminate them. Control the negotiation. Business owners often take for granted that if they bring a lot of value and sufficient leverage, they will strike a great deal. However, many other factors will influence where the negotiation ends up. Stay in control of what you want to ensure a positive outcome.

■ **Bring the process to the substance:** When an investor agrees to the funding amount, but before they sign the cheque, the process of due diligence must take place. Consider substance as the terms that make the final agreement. The process is how you will get to that agreement from where you stand today. Be ready and willing to thrash out details, objections, offers, and counteroffers.

■ The negotiating process calls for discussion and the ability to influence a range of factors that will affect the outcome of the deal. Ask the other party how much time their company will take to close the deal. Who else must get on board? Which factors can speed up or slow down the process? Are there any key milestones or dates to be aware of? Keep a track of simple things like: Who will be in the meeting? What's the agenda? If issues of importance to you are not being discussed in this meeting, when will they be discussed?

- You may not always get clear answers; sometimes questions can be considered premature. Try your best to reach a deep understanding of as many process elements as possible. Do this early on, to avoid a stumble on substance.

- Normalize the process. This entails an advance discussion about any factors that might risk the intended successful outcome. Why not share the typical barriers the involved parties need to overcome? It's common for parties to feel anxious, pessimistic, and out of place during negotiations. In such situations, parties need to agree to resolve the more serious issues first.

- Control the frame of negotiation (also called the psychological lens). This has a significant effect on where the negotiating parties end up, because it encompasses factors like whether parties are treating the discussion as a problem-solving exercise or a battle to be won. Are the parties meeting as equals, or is there a perceived difference in status from one or both sides? Are concessions expected or will they be seen as a sign of weakness?

- A successful negotiation seeks to control the outcome and adjusts the frame early on. Ideally, this could occur even before the substance of the deal is discussed.

- Use of proper visuals and images. The presence of visual aids in your pitch deck is crucial. Avoid being verbose, and use images and graphics of various kinds as much as possible. Avoid blurry or discolored images. Project a good visual appeal across your pitch deck, but do not over-use images, or arrange them sloppily without gridlines.

- Avoid clipart, generally speaking, as it tends to be cartoonish. Use a good high-res visual instead. Also avoid distracting backgrounds on the slides and images with watermarks.

THE TERM SHEET

Term sheets are difficult to understand, and you will certainly need help to understand all the provisions. It includes items like liquidation preference, anti-dilution protection, pay-or-play, drag-along rights, vesting schedules, no-shop clauses, and so on. Consult with a lawyer who is experienced with how to structure a VC deal. They can offer valuable input and help you understand what will be involved. Contact other companies in the VC firm's portfolio, to get a sense of what terms were negotiable, and why certain choices were made. Research and understand which terms were most consequential in the months and years after the deal.

The term sheet lays down the terms of the investment, along with the collateral which will be required. It details what the startup gives, and what it gets in return. It then lays out guidelines about how both parties will act, in order to protect the investment. A term sheet is generally provided after everything goes well with the founder's pitch deck. This may happen immediately or at a later meeting.

Term sheets can vary depending on the type of funding round, what is at stake, and who is involved in the negotiation. The term sheets for the seed round of funding are known to be much lighter than series A or beyond. Generally, the less at stake, the less complex the term sheet will be. However, the process can be simplified if using a third-party funding portal.

Typically, the investor provides the term sheet in the seed round. This can change if you take on multiple investors in later and larger rounds.

Common items in the term sheet include:

- Who issues the stock
- Type of collateral offered
- Valuation
- Amount offered
- Shares and price
- What happens in case of liquidation or IPO
- Voting rights
- Board seats
- Conversion options
- Anti-dilution provisions
- Investor's right to information
- Founder's obligation
- Who pays the legal expenses
- Non-disclosure requirements
- Rights to future investment
- Signatures

The term sheet is not in force without signatures. There is still due diligence to be performed. Parties sometimes do decide to go their separate ways without signing the term sheet.

Never talk badly of an investor just because you didn't like the deal. There are more deals to be found, and how you speak about an investor who didn't take the deal will affect the formation of your term sheet with the next investor. Once you shake hands on a deal, your word and reputation are the most valuable thing you have to offer.

Avoid thinking a term sheet is a done deal once it reaches your hands. Don't get comfortable and complacent. Increase your expenses and release funds wherever they are not immediately needed. Things can go wrong if the funding does not arrive on time, or the term sheet is never executed.

What to look out for in a term sheet, from a founder's perspective:

- Debt financing and convertible note terms that are too harsh and may end up leading to a bankruptcy for you. A controlling stake in the company which is large enough to replace you.
- Terms that can limit further fundraising
- Hot and short exit investors without realistic expectations.

Investors may tire the founder at this stage pretty easily, so it's important to be patient. Don't get restless and try to wrap things up too quickly. Many of the provisions in the term sheet may not make sense to you at the time but can put you, your co-founders, and your team in the wrong place if you handle them incorrectly.

Founders don't want greedy investors on board. Investors don't want unnecessary hassle and founders who just want to run away with the money. The term sheet is intended to develop a win-win relationship.

The rule of thumb is 20% dilution per round of financing. Avoid going over that amount. The life of a startup is long (hopefully) and you can never get back that dilution.

4

DOCUMENTING THE FUNDING

 ## COMPLETING DOCUMENTATION

Let's take a step back. We mentioned the "pit stops" that you must make before you get funded. These are summarized and ordered correctly below.

- Preliminary requirements, which include:
  - The correct, legal structure of the firm. This establishes the company as a legal entity—with all property in the name of the company.
  - Executive summary. A description of the core business.
  - Business plan. A detailed case of your business, including things like market analysis, financials, timelines, amount of investment sought, and what will be done with those funds.
  - Pitch deck. A brief summary of the company proposition, which may be presented or simply shared as reading material. Or both.
  - Share capitalization table. A solicitor will assist you with a draft of this table, to establish the structure of shares in the company before and after the

investment.

- Targeting investors. Research who your best-fit investors are.

- Networking. Expand your connections and reach out to potential investors.

■ Due diligence from the investor. When an investor expresses interest in making an investment in your company, they will begin their due diligence process. You will receive a preliminary request to share financial, corporate, and contractual status documentation.

The investor may request details like corporate information, budgets, forecasts, key supplier/customer, contracts in place, employees and employee contracts, intellectual property schedule, lease property schedule, a list of equipment owned (if applicable), details of other investors, shareholders, and bank loans. This will include any existing or future litigation, tax and VAT filings, insurance, and even data protection policies.

■ A term sheet will be needed, which (as you now know) is simply the terms of funding. This may show the terms of taking equity, convertible notes, or any other arrangement. It also lays down conditions to secure funding, including decisions regarding the dilution of shares and decision-making rights. The term sheet is not necessarily legally binding. Consider it as headline terms that both parties agree to before they get into minor details.

■ Next is the long-form documentation which implements the funding arrangement. This documentation generally includes:

- Shareholder or investment agreement. This details the agreed upon terms to be included on the term sheet. It tells how the control of the company is distributed.

- Vesting provisions. These may be crafted within the shareholder agreement. This protects the investors from key members of the founding team who might leave the company soon after investment. Certain shares vest over time, upon meeting certain milestones.

- Subscription agreement. This agreement details the business selling a certain number of shares to the investor at a certain price, and the willingness of the investor to pay that price.

- Articles of association. The articles that govern the operation once the company is funded.

This step confirms that the specific conditions to funding are met by each party, all the documents are prepared, and the terms fully agreed upon.

> *On the closing date, all the documents are signed and the transfer of funds and shares takes place.*

At this point, you have secured funding. It's time to show traction.

This step will vary in different countries. In the United States, the Enterprise Investment Scheme (EIS) and the Seed Enterprise Investment Scheme (SEIS) are tax reliefs. Early-stage investors are encouraged to invest in early startups via these schemes. A solicitor's advice is generally needed to ascertain qualifying criteria.

ACCOUNTING AND ADMINISTRATION

Immediately after you secure capital, there is some housekeeping to do. This includes the issuance of share certificates, updating the company's share register, and registering with the Companies House.

- You have to ensure your accounts and bookkeeping are immaculate and up-to-date. You will have to keep certain obligations in order to report your company's financial health.

- Getting funded will feel like something to celebrate, but don't congratulate the investor. It's time for you to show traction and hold to your word.

CONCLUSION:

THE WAY FORWARD
(LESSONS LEARNED)

Startups will need to secure multiple rounds of funding. It is important to look back on your journey, and recap what you've learned through the process. Contemplate what you could have done better, and how you can leverage the experience you've gotten out of the funding process so far.

We have covered a lot of information on how to get funded. However, money is not the only solution to your startup challenges. Money is only part of the larger equation.

Below are some salient points one learns from the first round of raising funds. Your relationship with your investor can get much, much better over time.

> *Your top priority is to keep your business healthy and growing.*

Don't chase funding just for the sake of it.

- Be ready to fail and get rejected. Try to reach out to best-fit investors.
- Look toward securing funds as gaining access to

successful people and their expertise.

- Have legal guidance on every document you sign. Don't rush into anything that makes you uncomfortable.

- Perform your due diligence on the investor you plan to work with. The goal has to be more than just "getting funded." What's the track record of the investor in demanding situations, particularly when companies are in rough weather and need their guidance and help?

- Understand common values and management styles. Sort out workflows, communication channels, and rhythm in advance.

- Getting funded is the time for action, not a point of celebration.

- Before you seek funding, get your business metrics in place.

- Lead and show traction. Investors don't care much about what the problem is or how it's getting solved. They just want to see things improving.

- Investors, particularly VCs, will not pass you to another investor even if they feel it's not a good fit.

I wish you success with your startup! You've got this.

CASE STUDIES

37COINS

Whenever a new technology comes along, there's almost always a goldrush to deliver services either using the technology or building upon it. That's certainly been the case with Bitcoin, where the community supporting it has faced many ups and downs since its launch in 2009. If you're not familiar with it, Bitcoin is a digital currency designed for use in peer-to-peer transactions.

One company that seemed like it was on top of the growing popularity of Bitcoin was 37Coins, a Bitcoin wallet that promised to make transactions on the Bitcoin blockchain easier and safer. In the world of Bitcoin, a wallet is an application that helps users securely hold virtual currencies. 37Coins wanted to take that concept even further by offering a number of tools to send Bitcoin and other fund types via SMS. But their ultimate goal was to provide banking services to unbanked cryptocurrency users.

Unfortunately, 37Coins' vision was never realized, and the company shuttered in 2014.

■ *What Went Wrong?*

Conducting Bitcoin transactions was originally very difficult, as the technology required more knowledge of blockchain technology than most ordinary users had.

Providing a user-friendly method for managing cryptocurrencies across both smartphones and older flip phones seemed like an excellent opportunity.

37Coins faced two large challenges that they were not able to overcome:

1) Implementing transfer technology across different regions that used different text messaging technologies was more difficult than the company originally imagined.

2) The firm's operational capital requirements outstripped the amount they were able to raise.[1]

While 37Coins was able to secure enough funding to launch an MVP, they ultimately weren't able to raise enough interest among investors to continue. While it's difficult to know precisely what went on behind closed doors, it's clear that their infrastructure costs were extremely high. For this reason, investors likely did not see 37Coins as a viable investment opportunity.

■ What Could They Have Done Better?

Maintaining servers all over the world is extremely costly, and 37Coins' plans of a global money transfer network may have been a little too ambitious.

It's likely the firm could have taken smaller steps and developed a more manageable roadmap in order to attract enough users to justify further investment. Scoring a win in a single market would have likely been more appealing to investors than a full-fledged global network, given the stage and uncertainty surrounding cryptocurrency technology and markets.

1: https://cointelegraph.com/news/37coinscom-shuts-down-bitcoin-operations

ADMAZELY

Founded in 2011, Admazely was a Danish startup that provided advertising tools for retargeting. Retargeting is an advertising technology that allows businesses to track website visitors and deliver ads to them on other websites. Admazely's technology helped businesses re-engage website visitors, and at the time it seemed like they were in the right place at the right time. Indeed, they even raised €600,000 in seed funding.[2] With a vision of going "instantly global," it seemed like everything was going right for Admazely.

But when sales didn't keep up with their cash burn rate, the founder raced to secure more funding. And unfortunately, his efforts were too late, the company ran out of money and had to close just three short years after it was founded.

■ *What Went Wrong?*

Founder Peter V. Therkildsen Schlegel wrote a highly

2: https://oresundstartups.com/startup-post-mortem-admazely-failed/

3: https://pschlegel.tumblr.com/post/62989782523/startup-failure-how- it-feels detailed post-mortem of his startup, wherein he detailed a perfect storm of events that led to the firm's downfall.[3] Chief among them was his overlooking raising any bridge funding between the seed and A rounds. By the time he had realized his mistake, it was likely too late and he was unable to raise the necessary bridge funds either through investment or loans. Add in emotional stresses from his own personal life, as well as work visa complications with key members of his sales team, and Admazely was unable to continue, shuttering in 2014.

■ *What Could They Have Done Better?*

Focusing on the right thing is challenging for any founder. It's understandable, given that founders are often pulled in multiple directions at once. Additionally, it's possible to be focused too far in the future while ignoring problems that are brewing in the present.

A better, sounder approach would have certainly been to spend a little more time planning the firm's finances. By his own account, the founder failed to recognize a key funding need before it was too late. Instead of planning for a bridge round, the founder was focused on prepping for his Series A round. A more thoughtful financing plan would have likely helped to keep Admazely afloat, allowing it to replace the staff members faster, while also providing the cushion needed to get to its Series A.

LAYERVAULT

As long as there are businesses, there will likely always be a need for graphic designers. While there are many types of designers with different specialties, they all likely have needs to manage and track files. These are large files, and most designers need to keep track of versions as they work with their clients through the design process. It can be tricky and challenging to do that without technology.

Which is why LayerVault was created. Founded in 2011, the platform was designed to provide design businesses with elegant, easy-to-use versioning tools along with unlimited file storage. Raising more than $500,000, the platform offered both a desktop and mobile applications.

Yet, the platform failed to gain enough traction among the design community and folded in 2014.

■ What Went Wrong?

As one designer put it, LayerVault "did do a job which was too vague and at the same time too specific."[4] A big challenge in any version control system is to support the types of files its users prefer. Unfortunately, there are many different design tools, each with different file types, and

---

4: https://www.designernews.co/stories/48017-the-legacy-of-layervault

LayerVault was not able to support all of them. Right away, this limitation potentially cut them off from large swaths of potential customers.

What's more, while the unlimited storage benefit was likely attractive to many designers, larger tech firms offer larger storage and file management solutions at a lower cost than LayerVault was able to match.

Lastly, LayerVault founder Kelly Sutton has said, "LayerVault was a company defined by its distractions." The company focused too much on developing complimentary products while not focusing enough on fundraising and growing its already existing platform.

■ *What Could They Have Done Better?*

Scaling is one of the most challenging tasks a startup needs to do. It's even more difficult when there are other competitive products in the marketplace; it's still an even greater challenge when one of your core benefits—unlimited storage—is being offered by huge tech firms with far deeper pockets. Perhaps the most important thing that LayerVault could have done is to build in support for a wider variety of file types. Staying focused on their core product would have likely resulted in gaining more traction with more users, and thus become a more appealing prospect for investors.